Walk on the Water

Janet E. Channell

Janet E. Channell

Copyright © 2010 Janet E. Channell. All rights reserved.

Writings contained herein are by the author unless otherwise stated.

No part of this publication may be reproduced, stored in a retrieval system or transmitted in any way by any means – electronic, mechanical, photocopy, recording or otherwise – without the prior permission of the copyright holder, except as provided by USA copyright law.

All Scriptures are taken from the King James Bible.

Cover photograph taken by Janet E. Channell.

ISBN# 978-1-61119-019-9

Printed in the United States of America.

Printed by Calvary Publishing
A Ministry of Parker Memorial Baptist Church
1902 East Cavanaugh Road
Lansing, Michigan 48910
www.CalvaryPublishing.org

www.calvarypublishing.org

Contents

Walk on the Water 7

Our Worldly Lives 13

Gift's of God 23

Helpmate or Heartache 27

Conformed to this World 37

We Shall Be Tempted 45

A Bound Root 51

Trials and Tribulations 57

Work as Unto the Lord 71

Our Lord's Return 77

America Land of the Free? 87

Our Pathway Home 93

Walk on the Water 105

References 109

Walk on the Water

Oh but to have the faith of a mustard seed we could move mountains. (Matthew 17:20) Have you ever just stopped and thought about that concept? To actually move a mountain with so powerful a faith? One would think this example set forth in the Bible is not to be taken literally but I believe that God's Word is all literal. It's just that our finite minds and hearts can't grasp hold of such a faith. Our feet are to heavily grounded upon this earth to allow us the spiritual heart and mind it takes too accept this possibility. Our souls are to earthbound in this human flesh.

How can an individual obtain such faith in this life we live? Perhaps not to move mountains or to walk on water as Peter did in Matthew 14:28-29. Peter had very great joy for a very short time as he trusted our Lord and stood on the water before Him. Oh to have such faith, inner peace and awe in our total beings while the whole world is falling apart around us. I look forward to asking Peter how he felt that day.

The "Last Days" are upon us and our time upon this earth and all that we do for our Lord will soon be over. As we look about us and see the changes in our nation, the life styles of society, and the course the world is taking, we have such little time left to serve our blessed Father who has given us life. We must use what time we have left to follow Him and obey His Word.

Jude 1:3-4, **"Beloved, when I gave all diligence to write unto you of the common salvation, it was needful for me to write unto you, and exhort *you* that ye should earnestly contend for the faith which was once delivered unto the saints. For there are certain men crept in unawares, who were before of old ordained to this condemnation, ungodly men, turning the grace of our God into lasciviousness, and denying the only Lord God, and our Lord Jesus Christ."**

My brother has a saying that I like concerning the Bible. Using the letters of the word "bible", he quotes "Basic Instruction Before Leaving Earth." That is exactly what the Bible is. Our basic instruction handbook and we should use it constantly every day, following our Lord in all He would have us to do.

Romans 10:17, **"So then faith *cometh* by hearing, and hearing by the word of God."**

Our hearts and minds should be focused on the future and our heavenly home. Not on this earthly place where Satan rules and reigns. Satan has this world totally engulfed now and sin dwells everywhere we look.

II Corinthians 6:2-7, "(**For he saith, I have heard thee in a time accepted, and in the day of salvation have I succoured thee: behold, now** *is* **the accepted time; behold, now** *is* **the day of salvation.**) Giving no offence in any thing, that the ministry be not blamed: But in all *things* approving ourselves as the ministers of God, in much patience, in afflictions, in necessities, in distresses, In stripes, in imprisonments, in tumults, in labours, in watchings, in fastings; By pureness, by knowledge, by longsuffering, by kindness, by the Holy Ghost, by love unfeigned, By the word of truth, by the power of God, by the armour of righteousness on the right hand and on the left,"

Verses 14-18, "Be ye not unequally yoked together with unbelievers: for what fellowship hath righteousness with unrighteousness? and what communion hath light with darkness? And what concord hath Christ with Belial? or what part hath he that believeth with an infidel? And what agreement hath the temple of God with idols? for ye are the temple of the living God; as God hath said, I will dwell in them, and walk in *them*; and I will be their God, and they shall be my people. Wherefore come out from among them, and be ye separate, saith the Lord, and touch not the unclean *thing*; and I will receive you, And will be

a Father unto you, and ye shall be my sons and daughters, saith the Lord Almighty."

As we see in these latter verses, our Lord exhorts us to live separate from the world for we are a precious people, children of the King. We should never let ourselves forget that we were bought with a price and that Christ gave His life for us on the Cross of Calvary. We should never be conformed to this world nor its' worldly ways. The lost of this world do not want any part of what we stand for and they will do all they can to pull us down and ruin our testimonies. We should never let them have the chance to get close enough to try. Protect our integrity and be the living witness that we should be, standing as an example of Christ before the world.

Romans 12:1-2, **"I beseech you therefore, brethren, by the mercies of God, that ye present your bodies a living sacrifice, holy, acceptable unto God, *which is* your reasonable service. And be not conformed to this world: but be ye transformed by the renewing of your mind, that ye may prove what *is* that good, and acceptable, and perfect, will of God."**

If we are serving the flesh and living after our worldly desires we will not have the strength to follow these scriptures. We must not allow Satan to lure us away and entrap us with a lot of worldly things that take our eyes off serving our Lord. Now, on the surface the things that we are engaged in may not seem to be sinful. Activities and organizations you may be a part of or places you go and things you do but do they take your eyes and minds off Christ? Are your time frames so full of the world that you don't have time to serve the Lord or attend Church? We'll go over several topics that hinder our service for our Lord and keep us from having a close personal relationship with our Father and Christ. My prayer is that we can draw closer to our Lord as the time for His return draws nearer. There's so little time left to serve Him and He is so very worthy of our praise, love and service.

Our Worldly Lives

Now we may want to say that we don't have worldly lives. After all, we are Christians saved by God's marvelous grace and we have turned away from the world. We attend Church and strive to follow His teachings.

However, the world has a way of coming into our homes in many avenues. The husband and many times the wife go out into the world to work and can't help but bring home this world with them. Just as the children also go out to school be it Public or Christian, and the world will be brought back into the home especially if it's a Public school. If it's a Christian school your blest and spared a great deal. Then we have our television sets, our computers, video games, and iPods. The children can get so wrapped up in the latter two items that you won't see them for hours.

If we are a modern family it seems that the parents feel compelled to encourage their children to participate in many extra curricular activities outside the home such as sports, cheerleading, ballet, band, and clubs.

Now I realize that these are good social outlets for our children and help to make them well rounded, especially band and sports. We all want our children to be socially mature and able to interact as well rounded individuals as they grow up. However, there are many ways this can be done without subjecting them to other worldly children where they will learn a great deal more than we would like.

Colossians 2:8, **"Beware lest any man spoil you through philosophy and vain deceit, after the tradition of men, after the rudiments of the world, and not after Christ."**

Sinful ways and rebellious attitudes can come when they see how loose a life style other children live. Habits can be picked up that we don't want in our children. There is also the inevitable practice that falls on the mid-week service or keeps the family from attending other special church meetings that are being held.

All this happens subtlety. You don't think about it at the time. Everyone is doing it. It's good for the kids - helps build character. It's only later on that we may find it wasn't quite the character we were hoping to be built.

Romans 6:15-17, **"What then? shall we sin, because we are not under the law, but under grace? God forbid. Know ye not, that to whom ye yield yourselves servants to obey, his servants ye are to whom ye obey; whether of sin unto death, or of obedience unto righteousness But**

Our Worldly Lives

God be thanked, that ye were the servants of sin, but ye have obeyed from the heart that form of doctrine which was delivered you."

The media is so very full of the worldly woes and ways. It will fill our hearts and minds with sadness and tribulation. Politics alone can drive many Christians into evil thoughts and despair.

The computer brings us the internet which opens the world to us through its monitor. Any topic we wish to find out about can be learned at the touch of a few buttons. This is especially dangerous with children in the house and their freedom to the internet. They may be learning a great deal about a great many subjects that they are far too young to be aware of. Sinful impressions once seen, heard, or read cannot be erased from their minds. Innocence is lost when it could have been prevented. Our young people should be spared the filth of this world as much as possible.

Now we have the video games in which young people become absorbed. If we are not careful these games they play and fill their minds with can be full of violence, foul language and sex. The games are rated the first being "Everyone"; rated for all children to play without too much fear of emotional damage. The second is "Teen"; in which you have descriptions of language, violence and or blood depending on how bad this particular game may be.

Third you have "Mature 17+"; which is followed by descriptions of blood and gore, drug references, and intense violence. We as parents can do our best to make sure they only play the general games but what do they play when they are at their friends house? We can't be with them every moment. The violence in these games can desensitize them. They will become insensitive to these actions and after a time death and murder will not be as serious as it once was to them. Not only in these games but television programs and action movies where violence is glorified. We as parents must guard our children and help to guide them as they grow. They are our responsibility.

John 14:27, "**Peace I leave with you, my peace I give unto you: not as the world giveth, give I unto you. Let not your heart be troubled, neither let it be afraid.**"

Philippians 4:7, "**And the peace of God, which passeth all understanding, shall keep your hearts and minds through Christ Jesus.**"

The modern home of the Christian Family has become so very busy today. You accommodate the active lives of the family scheduling in band and sports practice and the club meetings. Before you know it you meet yourselves coming and going. Time is taken up so fully that the husband and wife pass each other at the door as they rush to pick up this one or that one from a practice or club meeting. Meals are seldom shared together as a family unit and Mom and Dad sit back exhausted wondering if it's worth the trouble.

During all this coming and going, how much time during the week has each family member spent with the Lord? How much Bible reading was done? Which hour was set aside for family devotions? Mom, if your working outside the home as well as keeping up with the time frames of all the other family members, you are probably ready to fall on your face about now. Why the "Rat-Race"? What is gained? I'm afraid the only one who has gained in this family is Satan and he's having a field day keeping your household in a whirl while no one can focus on the one who should be center of the household - that being Christ! A family can't serve the Lord in this manner.

We ladies are to be keepers of the home. After WWII women were able to return to their homes where they had been content to be before working in the factories. But Satan had given them a taste of independence and they liked it. This was also the era in which women began wearing slacks more regularly.

Deuteronomy 6:7, **"And thou shalt teach them diligently unto thy children, and shalt talk of them when thou sittest in thine house, and when**

thou walkest by the way, and when thou liest down, and when thou risest up."

This verse alone shows us that a mother has to be in the home the entire day teaching her children about our Lord. In order for a mother to truly know and understand her children she must be with them, watching them in all their various moods. We won't know just when something is deeply bothering them or that they are troubled about an issue unless we are used to seeing all their normal actions and reactions. It takes time to get to know their nuances and demeanor to really see if they are content or being bothered by something. Their body language can speak louder than words but we mothers must be there to see it.

God tells us He wants us to stay in our home, taking care of our families. He didn't create us to handle the stress that must be faced and stood up to in the arena of the world. Women have a great many increased illnesses such as heart disease, nervous disorders, cancer, such as lung cancer from the increased number of women smoking heavily and the number of women committing suicides as they cannot adapt to all the work load put upon them. God has always had a set pattern in which we as His servants are to lead our lives and we women are to maintain the homes as our husbands go out into the workplace confronting the world's affairs. Let us

Our Worldly Lives

honor God by obeying His Word.

Now how do we get back to where we ought to be with the Lord? We can start by repenting of leaving our Lord behind. Then start to remove some of the extra activities that are going on in the home. Bring the chicks back under the wing a bit. Instead of band your child could learn to play piano. Social interaction can be fulfilled by going to Church Conference's and Special services where your children can meet other children who are also saved and of the same background and faith. Daughters can do baby-sitting instead of working at a dress shop or fast food restaurant. It is best for them to learn to stay in the home and practice how to run a home for the day when they too, grow up and have families of their own.

Titus 2:3, **"The aged women likewise, that *they be* in behaviour as becometh holiness, not false accusers, not given to much wine, teachers of good things;"**

I Timothy 5:14-15, **"I will therefore that the younger women marry, bear children, guide the house, give none occasion to the adversary to speak reproachfully. For some are already turned aside after Satan."**

If you know that the sin of neglect is present in your life or a sin that is not mentioned here but felt in your heart, repentance is called for. Our lives are to be lived for the Lord, not for earthly gain or self-acclaim. There is the sin of disbelief, not for salvation but of faith in God to supply all your needs and care for you in all ways. You fail to have the faith that He will always be there for you and your family. Our Lord can do miraculous things in your life.

If you work outside the home and feel you can't stop for financial reasons you must have faith in God to supply your financial need while you obey His will in staying within the home. Step out by faith and trust in our Lord to supply all your need. You may have to down-size and live on a smaller plain than your used to but God will bless. God blesses faithfulness.

Isaiah 26:3, **"Thou wilt keep *him* in perfect peace, *whose* mind *is* stayed *on thee:* because he trusteth in thee."**

Hebrews 11:1-3, **"Now faith is the substance of things hoped for, the evidence of things not seen. For by it the elders obtained a good report. Through faith we understand that the worlds were framed by the word of God, so that things which are seen were not made of things which do appear."**

James 2:17-20, **"Even so faith, if it hath not works, is dead, being alone. Yea, a man may say, Thou hast faith, and I have works: shew me thy faith without thy works, and I will shew thee** my faith by my works. Thou believest that there is one God; thou doest well: the devils also believe, and tremble. But wilt thou know, O vain man, that faith without works is dead?"

Gift's of God

Romans 12:6-17, "Having then gifts differing according to the grace that is given to us, whether prophecy, *let us prophesy* according to the proportion of faith; Or ministry, *let us wait* on *our* ministering: or he that teacheth, on teaching; Or he that exhorteth, on exhortation: he that giveth, *let him do it* with simplicity; he that ruleth, with diligence; he that sheweth mercy, with cheerfulness. *Let* love be without dissimulation. Abhor that which is evil; cleave to that which is good. Be kindly affectioned one to another with brotherly love; in honour preferring one another; Not slothful in business; fervent in spirit; serving the Lord; Rejoicing in hope; patient in tribulation; continuing instant in prayer; Distributing to the necessity of saints; given to hospitality. Bless them which persecute you: bless, and curse not. Rejoice with them that do rejoice, and weep with them that weep. *Be* of the same mind one toward another. Mind not high things, but condescend to men of low estate. Be not wise in your own conceits. Recompense to no man evil for evil. Provide things honest in the sight of all men."

James 1:17, "**Every good gift and every perfect gift is from above, and cometh down from the Father of lights, with whom is no variableness, neither shadow of turning.**"

His Spirit has blessed each and everyone of us with a gift and we are to enhance each one of these gifts and use them to the best of our ability so that we bring honor and glory to our Lord. Some of us may feel that we do not have a gift given to us because we cannot preach the Word, play a piano, be a teacher or organize large groups for a fellowship. But there are a great many more types of gifts that God gives His Children other than those we might consider to be talents. We might have a loving and giving spirit or perhaps we're a prayer warrior or one who can always be counted upon to listen to people's problems so others can vent and heal. These are tremendous gifts indeed.

If you are not sure of the gift or gifts which God has bestowed upon you just ask Him and quietly listen to what He tells you. He will let you know exactly what your gift is so you can use it for His honor and glory.

Philippians 2:12-13, "**Wherefore, my beloved, as ye have always obeyed, not as in my presence only, but now much more in my absence, work out your own salvation with fear and trembling. For it is God which worketh in you both to will** and to do of *his* good pleasure."

I Thessalonians 5:15-24, "**See that none render evil for evil unto any** *man***; but ever follow that which is good, both among yourselves, and to all** *men***. Rejoice evermore. Pray without ceasing. In every thing give thanks: for this is the will of God in Christ Jesus concerning you. Quench not the Spirit. Despise not prophesyings. Prove all things; hold fast that which is good. Abstain from all appearance of evil. And the very God of peace sanctify you wholly; and** *I pray God* **your whole spirit and soul and body be preserved blameless unto the coming of our Lord Jesus Christ. Faithful** *is* **he that calleth you, who also will do** *it*.**"**

Helpmate or Heartache

I would like to examine a few areas that might be a cause of separation that we may suffer from our Lord. One of them might be the inability to submit to our husbands. In this day and age learned behaviors can take hold of us and we may be unaware that we are not showing our husbands the respect that our Lord would expect us too. I will try to reveal through the scriptures what I mean by that statement.

I know that we may say that we are not for woman's liberation but Satan has silently worked his way into our lives and our actions and reactions - especially with our husband's, revealing just how good a job he has done. We look at our husbands and may love them dearly but out of a learned behavior, we often respond to them or make comments in what we feel is a joking manner. However, in reality it sounds like a belittlement in which we are degrading our husband, many times in front of other people. This may be done because of an ill-feeling due to something he said or did to hurt us. Or it might just be a bad habit that we've grown used to and do it without thinking. Either way and for whatever reason, putting our husbands down or setting them straight on an issue with such open remarks or rebukes must never be done! As we go on I'll show you through the scriptures why this is so very important to adhere to.

If we feel we have something to tell our husbands we should tell them quietly.

I Peter 3:1-6, **"Likewise, ye wives, *be* in subjection to your own husbands; that, if any obey not the word, they also may without the word be won by the conversation of the wives; While they behold your chaste conversation *coupled* with fear. Whose adorning let it not be that outward *adorning* of plaiting the hair, and of wearing of gold, or of putting on of apparel; But *let it be* the hidden man of the heart, in that which is not corruptible, *even the ornament* of a meek and quiet spirit, which is in the sight of God of great price. For after this manner in the old time the holy women also, who trusted in God, adorned themselves, being in subjection unto their own husbands: Even as Sara obeyed Abraham, calling him lord: whose daughters ye are, as long as ye do well, and are not afraid with any amazement."**

Even as Sara obeyed-(to conform to a command or authority)

Calling him lord-(supreme in authority, as a respectful title: God, Lord, Master, Sir.)

And are not afraid-(in awe of, revere, fear exceedingly)

With any amazement-(alarm, to scare, frighten)

Please read these scriptures carefully and truly look at what they are saying to us. Chaste conversation is referring to our behavior. Chaste is to be innocent, modest, perfect, clean, pure. Whose adorning is the **"...*ornament* of a meek and quiet spirit, which is in the sight of God of great price."** Does she sound like she'd belittle her husband in public? The verses go on to express how Sara called Abraham lord. Sara had great respect for Abraham and called him lord. She had a meek and quiet spirit which God loves in His daughters. Sara obeyed Abraham and was under subjection to him. As the scriptures tell us, "whose daughters ye are as long as ye do well, and are not afraid with any amazement." This means that it will take special grace to follow Sara in her example of submission and in reference to Abraham as lord. This is because so few are doing so and those who will stand up and be strong in our Lord, obeying His Word, will not fit in with the norm in this world. Those who do, will be God's daughters indeed.

Subjection is usually more difficult for women who are younger or out in the work force more. Liberation and its effects are easily absorbed as we witness the world around us.

Malachi 3:6, **"For I *am* the LORD, I change**

not…"

His Word will always mean exactly what it says, no matter what age we are living in.

Ephesians 5:22, **"Wives, submit yourselves unto your own husbands, as unto the Lord."**

Submit-(to obey, be under obedience; put under, subdue.)

The word Lord means Master. Just as we seen in I Peter 3:6 where Sara obeyed Abraham calling him Lord. We see that this very same word used throughout the New Testament and is meant to mean our "Lord" as well. It is the same degree of subjection as we give to our Lord and Christ when used in reference to our husbands. Subjection as found in such verses as II Corinthians 9:13, **"…unto the gospel of Christ…"** Ephesians 5:24, **"…as the church is subject unto Christ…"** Hebrews 12:9, **"…unto the Father of spirits…"** and James 4:7, **"Submit yourselves therefore to God…"**

To be in subjection to our Lord God is something we understand and freely acknowledge. However, when we think that this same depth of subjection is meant to be acknowledged toward our husbands also, it takes this teaching to a whole new level.

Some may find this very difficult to grasp or even to accept. But God's word does not change. It is a Biblical practice that God held from the very beginning. It started with Eve in the Garden of Eden.

Genesis 3:16, "**...and thy desire *shall be* to thy husband, and he shall rule over thee.**"

Desire-(sense of stretching out after; longing - desire.)

Rule-(dominion, reign, have power)

Ladies this desire was given to us by God. He put this natural desire within us women from the very beginning of time. We have a natural God given need and tendency to reach out and long for our husband's strength and headship over us.

I Corinthians 11:3, "**But I would have you know, that the head of every man is Christ; and the head of the woman *is* the man; and the head of Christ *is* God.**"

This is God's placement of mankind. Men have the Federal Headship over women. We were created to be their helpmates in Genesis 2, when God said that man should not be alone and He created a companion to share his life with him.

Ephesians 5:22-23, "**Wives, submit yourselves unto your own husbands, as unto the Lord. For the husband is the head of the wife, even as Christ is the head of the church: and he is the saviour of the body.**" (Also Colossians 3:18)

Submission is needful as we have seen throughout these verses. When I was first saved I found subjection a bit hard to swallow. I'm a very strong willed person and I have a lot of opinions I like to share. So when I was first taught the concept of submission I realized I was to be subject to my husband-a husband who had a great many flaws which I could see. Now he had to be in subjection to Christ who is faultless. Now this had me sitting up and taking notice. I had some very good thoughts that I felt were very needful and could help my husband greatly as he served our Lord. Have any of you dear sisters ever felt that way? I soon learned that he didn't want my help and the more I heard subjection taught the more I realized that to be in subjection is to be quiet a great deal of the time. This was a very hard truth for me to physically concur. I literally had to bit my tongue until it bled to keep my mouth shut. But I believed the scriptures and I believed God when He said for me to do it. My submission was at first aimed toward my respect for God. Little by little I learned that submission was my way of showing my great love and respect for my husband also.

Over the years I have grown to learn a great deal about my ideas and the fact that I am wrong on many occasions. I tend to think with my heart and not my head. I now listen to my husband's wisdom and find that he is right far more than not. This is not to say that he does not listen to me when I have thoughts of my own. He is very good about asking my opinion. And when I tell him it is in a pleasant conversation. We respect each other and there is no need to raise our voices or hurt each others feelings.

When you come upon a time when you see that talking to your husband won't help, just take the situation to our Lord and tell Him all about it. He cares what you think and wants us to share our thoughts and feelings with Him. Besides He can do something about the problem. There is an added benefit to being able to talk to God instead of our husbands at times.

Remember that we said man has the natural headship? Well, when we women open our mouths to "help" our husbands, they have an inner ear that often will automatically turn off when we begin to be too expressive. They simply will not listen. Call it pride of man if you will but it is God given. When we relax and trust God to lead and direct our husbands, letting God do the talking, we will find everything will be in harmony. When we rest in our Lord and His wisdom to take care of a matter we can know the situation will be fine.

Genesis 2:23-24, **"And Adam said, This *is* now bone of my bones, and flesh of my flesh: she shall be called Woman, because she was taken out of Man. Therefore shall a man leave his father and his mother, and shall cleave unto his wife: and they shall be one flesh."**

Cleave-(abide fast together, be joined, follow

close hard after, keep fast.)

Mark 10:8, **"And they twain shall be one flesh: so then they are no more twain, but one flesh."**

These scriptures stress the oneness that a husband and wife are to become. No longer two individuals with independent lives but a bonded unit acting as a whole. Today couples tend to act independently of each other. That is not how our Lord wanted our married lives to be.

We must strive to think in our hearts and minds as one, putting the other first and caring for each other more than life itself. My husband and I have been married 41 years and we are happier now than we have ever been. As time goes by the oneness should take hold and a true bonding should take place in your lives.

Ecclesiastes 9:9, **"Live joyfully with the wife whom thou lovest all the days of the life of thy vanity, which he hath given thee under the sun, all the days of thy vanity: for that *is* thy portion in *this* life, and in thy labour which thou takest under the sun."**

Ephesians 5:28, **"So ought men to love their wives as their own bodies. He that loveth his wife loveth himself."**

Colossians 3:19, **"Husbands, love *your* wives, and be not bitter against them."**

Ephesians 5:25, **"Husbands, love your wives,**

even as Christ also loved the church, and gave himself for it;"

Our husbands are to love us as Christ loves the church. And how does Christ show His love, care, and concern for His Church? By always being with her, directing and encouraging her and when needed - correcting her. This is how earnestly our husbands are to love and care for us, treating us like precious gems to be treasured.

This brings us to our central text in I Peter 3:7, **"Likewise, ye husbands, dwell with *them* according to knowledge, giving honour unto the wife, as unto the weaker vessel, and as being heirs together of the grace of life; that your prayers be not hindered."**

Knowledge-(knowing)

Giving honour-(esteem, dignity itself, precious price)

As we have already seen earlier in this chapter, the husband is to esteem his wife very highly as a precious jewel. He values her as a God given companion who is to help him in contributing to their needs and well being, sharing the grace of life together as one.

There has been a great deal said concerning subjection and all the areas surrounding it. The seriousness of the headship as seen in Ephesians 5:22, and I Peter 3:6. These scriptures are not to be taken lightly. Oh, we may not go about calling our husbands lord but we must remember that in God's eyes they are and they should be in ours as well, as we look at them through the eyes of love and the respect due them. We ladies have a great realm with so many eyes upon us. This realm should be the home which is our sphere - our center, our base from which the whole family has a solid foundation. Are we as we should be before our Lord concerning this topic of subjection? Are there areas in which we need to repent of? Have we made our homes the stable oasis for our family to come home to? I know that as a whole, none of us are as we should be before God on these issues. Our flesh gets in our way and we're only human. But we must strive to follow our Lord and His will in our lives. The closeness that is to be gained and the rich fellowship is so sweet when we are well with God.

Conformed to this World

Life in our Lord can truly be wonderful but we can be to conformed to this world and it's worldly ways that serving Him may be very hard to do and not come very naturally. The world has invaded our lives to such a point that we don't realize how little time we spend even thinking of our Lord or considering His desires for our lives.

Luke 18:8 **"I tell you that he will avenge them speedily. Nevertheless when the Son of man cometh, shall he find faith on the earth?"**

Romans 12:1-2, **"I beseech you therefore, brethren, by the mercies of God, that ye present your bodies a living sacrifice, holy, acceptable unto God, *which is* your reasonable service. And be not conformed to this world: but be ye transformed by the renewing of your mind, that ye may prove what *is* that good, and acceptable, and perfect, will of God."**

We are to live our lives transformed by renewing our minds, reading our Bibles daily and praying, staying close to our Lord. Note that this is our reasonable service as we mentioned before. Just reasonable service no more and no less. But because of Satan we have taken our eyes off Christ so much that serving Him so automatically is beyond comprehension.

II Timothy 2:15-16 & 19-22, **"Study to shew thyself approved unto God, a workman that needeth not to be ashamed, rightly dividing the word of truth. But shun profane *and* vain babblings: for they will increase unto more ungodliness…Nevertheless the foundation of God standeth sure, having this seal, The Lord knoweth them that are his. And, Let every one that nameth the name of Christ depart from iniquity. But in a great house there are not only vessels of gold and of silver, but also of wood and of earth; and some to honour, and some to dishonour. If a man therefore purge himself from these, he shall be a vessel unto honour, sanctified, and meet for the master's use, *and* prepared unto every good work. Flee also youthful lusts: but follow righteousness, faith, charity, peace, with them that call on the Lord out of a pure heart."**

James 3:8 **"But the tongue can no man tame; *it is* an unruly evil, full of deadly poison."**

Being set apart for our Lord in all areas of our lives includes the taming of our tongues. Watching our speech and making sure that it does not dishonor our Lord. Bad language looks bad on anyone but most of all on someone who claims to be a child of God. I once was told that a person who used cursing was a person who was not intelligent enough to know how to use better language. Whatever the reason, it should not be found on the lips of a child of God. It does not stop at bad language. Lies, backbiting, and causing strife are all things which we as children of God must not do.

Proverbs 6:16-19, **"These six *things* doth the LORD hate: yea, seven *are* an abomination unto him: A proud look, a lying tongue, and hands that shed innocent blood, An heart that deviseth wicked imaginations, feet that be swift in running to mischief, A false witness *that* speaketh lies, and he that soweth discord among brethren."**

Our whole purpose in our Christian life is to bring honor and glory to God in everything that we do. This means obeying what the Bible tells us and following His Words. All that is not done for Christ will be burnt up and a total waste of time. If we live our lives in any way that does not follow God's Word, glorifying Him by obeying His teachings, those works will be burnt up and totally done in vain. Where is the sense in that? Do we want our lives to account for nothing when they could account for everything? If we obeyed God we would receive pure joy and peace in our hearts that passes all understanding serving Him with our lives.

Being sanctified one step at a time, little by little,

setting aside our sins and becoming more like Christ would have us be everyday. I Peter 1:2, **"Elect according to the foreknowledge of God the Father, through sanctification of the Spirit, unto obedience and sprinkling of the blood of Jesus Christ: Grace unto you, and peace, be multiplied."**

Philippians 2:1-5, **"If *there be* therefore any consolation in Christ, if any comfort of love, if any fellowship of the Spirit, if any bowels and mercies, Fulfil ye my joy, that ye be likeminded, having the same love, *being* of one accord, of one mind. *Let* nothing *be done* through strife or vainglory; but in lowliness of mind let each esteem other better than themselves. Look not every man on his own things, but every man also on the things of others. Let this mind be in you, which was also in Christ Jesus:"**

Why were we saved? For what purpose? Ephesians 3:11-20, **"According to the eternal purpose which he purposed in Christ Jesus our Lord: In whom we have boldness and access with confidence by the faith of him. Wherefore I desire that ye faint not at my tribulations for you, which is your glory. For this cause I bow my knees unto the Father of our Lord Jesus Christ, Of whom the whole family in heaven and earth is named, That he would grant you, according to the riches of his glory, to be strengthened with might by his**

Spirit in the inner man; That Christ may dwell in your hearts by faith; that ye, being rooted and grounded in love, May be able to comprehend with all saints what *is* the breadth, and length, and depth, and height; And to know the love of Christ, which passeth knowledge, that ye might be filled with all the fulness of God. Now unto him that is able to do exceeding abundantly above all that we ask or think, according to the power that worketh in us,"

Philippians 2:5-11, "**Let this mind be in you, which was also in Christ Jesus: Who, being in the form of God, thought it not robbery to be equal with God: But made himself of no reputation, and took upon him the form of a servant, and was made in the likeness of men: And being found in fashion as a man, he humbled himself, and became obedient unto death, even the death of the cross. Wherefore God also hath highly exalted him, and given him a name which is above every name: That at the name of Jesus every knee should bow, of *things* in heaven, and *things* in earth, and *things* under the earth; And *that* every tongue should confess that Jesus Christ *is* Lord, to the glory of God the Father."**

Christ gave Himself on the Cross of Calvary for us and we should be willing to turn our backs to the world and serve Him while there is still time. He is going to return so very soon and our time of service for Him will be over. Let's let go of all those worldly extra curricular activities that have taken up our time wasting it on things that will never matter. When our eyes, hearts and minds should be upon our Lord where our eternity lies.

Philippians 2:12-17, **"Wherefore, my beloved, as ye have always obeyed, not as in my presence only, but now much more in my absence, work out your own salvation with fear and trembling. For it is God which worketh in you both to will and to do of** *his* **good pleasure. Do all things without murmurings and disputings: That ye may be blameless and harmless, the sons of God, without rebuke, in the midst of a crooked and perverse nation, among whom ye shine as lights in the world; Holding forth the word of life; that I may rejoice in the day of Christ, that I have not run in vain, neither laboured in vain. Yea, and if I be offered upon the sacrifice and service of your faith, I joy, and rejoice with you all."**

If you desire an item or situation in your life that God hasn't provided and it is just, than He will provide or not provide according to our good. He knows what is best for each and every one of us and will supply what He knows we need. If we do not receive what we feel we want very badly there is a very good reason for it. We must trust God's wisdom in the matter and be content with what we have. For whatever reason God does not see fit to give it to us and we should be content with life without the item or situation whatever it may be. If we are not, it is lust on our part even if the item wanted is good and reasonable.

Psalms 33:4-5, **"For the word of the LORD is right; and all his works *are done* in truth. He loveth righteousness and judgment: the earth is full of the goodness of the LORD."**

II Timothy 1:8-14, **"Be not thou therefore ashamed of the testimony of our Lord, nor of me his prisoner: but be thou partaker of the afflictions of the gospel according to the power of God; Who hath saved us, and called *us* with an holy calling, not according to our works, but according to his own purpose and grace, which was given us in Christ Jesus before the world began, But is now made manifest by the appearing of our Saviour Jesus Christ, who hath abolished death, and hath brought life and immortality to light through the gospel: Whereunto I am appointed a preacher, and an apostle, and a teacher of the Gentiles. For the which cause I also suffer these things: nevertheless I am not ashamed: for I know whom I have believed, and am persuaded that he is able to keep that which I have committed unto him against that day. Hold fast the form** of sound words, which thou hast heard of me, in faith and love which is in Christ Jesus. That good thing which was committed unto thee keep by the Holy Ghost which dwelleth in us."

We Shall Be Tempted

James 1:13-15, **"Let no man say when he is tempted, I am tempted of God: for God cannot be tempted with evil, neither tempteth he any man: But every man is tempted, when he is drawn away of his own lust, and enticed. Then when lust hath conceived, it bringeth forth sin: and sin, when it is finished, bringeth forth death."**

Temptations are not of God and when we are drawn toward sin through our own lust and enticed, giving place to these temptations, sin is brought forth. This sin when it is finished brings forth death.

I Corinthians 10:13, **"There hath no temptation taken you but such as is common to man: but God *is* faithful, who will not suffer you to be tempted above that ye are able; but will with the temptation also make a way to escape, that ye may be able to bear *it*."**

Matthew 26:41, **"Watch and pray, that ye enter not into temptation: the spirit indeed *is* willing, but the flesh *is* weak."**

We are not to fear for there will not be a temptation that can overtake us in this manner. For God has said He will always give us a way to escape the temptation so we can bear it. There will always be a way out. All we have to do is look to our Lord and grasp a hold of it and take the escape offered unto us. The flesh would have us ignore the escape route. In fact if we look through the eyes of flesh we will not look for the escape route at all. So our hearts must be open to our Lord and we must have a desire within us to serve Him in order to take the escape.

Galatians 6:1-2, **"Brethren, if a man be overtaken in a fault, ye which are spiritual, restore such an one in the spirit of meekness; considering thyself, lest thou also be tempted. Bear ye one another's burdens, and so fulfil the law of Christ."**

If we have a sister who has fallen prey to a sin we should help her and lift her up. We must realize that but for the grace of God go we all. We must help each other as we find ourselves stumbling in our weaknesses. No one else will ever help us. The world will rejoice when they see us fall into sin. They will be most happy to see us fail in our witness for Christ. We are all we have to help each other.

Hebrews 4:14-16, **"Seeing then that we have a great high priest, that is passed into the heavens, Jesus the Son of God, let us hold fast *our* profession. For we have not an high priest which cannot be touched with the feeling of our infirmities; but was in all points tempted like as *we*** *are, yet* **without sin. Let us therefore come boldly unto the throne of grace, that we may obtain mercy, and find grace to help in time of need."**

Christ felt all things that we go through here on earth. He knows what and how we feel in any given situation. We truly are never alone in anything we live through while we are here on earth. When we pray and ask Him for help He knows exactly how and what way to help. We have a wonderful Saviour.

I Corinthians 2:9-12 & 14, **"But as it is written, Eye hath not seen, nor ear heard, neither have entered into the heart of man, the things which God hath prepared for them that love him. But God hath revealed** *them* **unto us by his Spirit: for the Spirit searcheth all things, yea, the deep things of God. For what man knoweth the things of a man, save the spirit of man which is in him? even so the things of God knoweth no man, but the Spirit of God. Now we have received, not the spirit of the world, but the spirit which is of God; that we might know the things that are freely given to us of God…But the natural man receiveth not the things of the Spirit of God: for they are foolishness unto him: neither can he know** *them***, because they are spiritually discerned."**

The Word of God is freely given unto us to accept and believe. However, if we do not have the Holy Spirit within us to direct and instruct us, opening up the scriptures for our learning we will never be able to understand what they mean.

Faith starts at the Word of God. Without faith in the Word there can be no faith in the salvation so freely given to us by the gift of Christ. For we must believe that the Bible truly comes from God and is His Word to us in order to continue on and believe the rest of the plan of salvation and the acceptance of Christ as our Saviour.

Ephesians 2:4-6 & 8-9, **"But God, who is rich in mercy, for his great love wherewith he loved us, Even when we were dead in sins, hath quickened us together with Christ, (by grace ye are saved;) And hath raised *us* up together, and made *us* sit together in heavenly *places* in Christ Jesus … FFor by grace are ye saved through faith; and that not of yourselves: *it is* the gift of God: Not of works, lest any man should boast."**

Romans 10:8-13 & 17-18, **"But what saith it? The word is nigh thee, *even* in thy mouth, and in thy heart: that is, the word of faith, which we preach; That if thou shalt confess with thy mouth the Lord Jesus, and shalt believe in thine heart that God hath raised him from the dead, thou shalt be saved. For with the heart man believeth unto righteousness; and with the mouth confession is made unto salvation. For the scripture saith, Whosoever believeth on him shall not** be ashamed. For there is no difference between the Jew and the Greek: for the same Lord over all is rich unto all that call upon him. For whosoever shall call upon the name of the Lord shall be saved...So then faith *cometh* by hearing, and hearing by the word of God. But I say, Have they not heard? Yes verily, their sound went into all the earth, and their words unto the ends of the world."

Psalms 146:5, "**Happy** *is he* **that** *hath* **the God of Jacob for his help, whose hope** *is* **in the LORD his God:**"

Our faith is founded in the Word of God in the revelation of our Holy Spirit and we are drawn closer to our Lord. Learning of Him and accepting what His Son has done on the Cross for us in the forgiveness of sins.

A Bound Root

Psalms 34:14, **"Depart from evil, and do good; seek peace, and pursue it."**

Peace is a tangible thing - something that we must work at in order to obtain. Our hearts and minds must be clear of the world in order to obtain this peace God gives us.

Hebrews 12:14-17, **"Follow peace with all *men*, and holiness, without which no man shall see the Lord: Looking diligently lest any man fail of the grace of God; lest any root of bitterness springing up trouble *you*, and thereby many be defiled; Lest there *be* any fornicator, or profane person, as Esau, who for one morsel of meat sold his birthright. For ye know how that afterward, when he would have inherited the blessing, he was rejected: for he found no place of repentance, though he sought it carefully with tears."** Also see James 3:13-18.

A bitter root is a sore pain deep within which will fester and grow larger like a cancer, killing all the cells around it. What is a bitter root? It can be many things to many people but the result is always the same. It keeps us from serving the Lord. Bitterness grieves the Holy Spirit and keeps us hard hearted in attitude, (I deserve to feel bitter). Bitterness defiles and blackens, causing our vision to be obscured, turning us backward rather then forward to Christ.

The bitter root can be caused by a wrong doing, hurt feelings or a terrible loss as something is taken away from us. There can be any one of a hundred different causes for a bitter root but the outcome is the destroying of our inner peace, joy and spirit. This type of pain is so very harmful for it goes throughout our life, living within our memories and subconscious effecting all facets of our life and how we interact with other people. Everything we say and feel will be negative and we will bring down those about us. We will be difficult to be around when we have a bitter root.

After a prolonged time a bitter root can literally make people ill as they neglect themselves because of their depression and poor feelings caused by the bitter root. What can be done? Just as in our verses in reference to Esau. He cried over his lost birthright but once it was lost there was nothing he could do to get it back. A person in his case could sit in self-pity and let the cancer of the root grow out of all proportions. Or he could accept the fact that the treasure was lost to him. Acknowledge the situation as it is and repent for not trusting God in the first place and in allowing the root to take hold. Repent, accept God's wisdom and will in the matter and go

A Bound Root

on with life. You see, nothing happens in our lives that God does not know about. God knew all about Esau and allowed him to lose the birthright because of his lack of strength and desire.

Ephesians 4:32, **"And be ye kind one to another, tenderhearted, forgiving one another, even as God for Christ's sake hath forgiven you."**

As we see in the verse **"…even as God for Christ's sake hath forgiven you."** God gave up all for us in the person of His beloved Son, Jesus Christ. He has shown us a tremendous example to follow. Forgiveness costs a great deal because it asks us to release all the bitterness, pain, anger, and resentment we have stored up for so long. Release it and forgive all the accounts of those who have harmed us, allowing their debt to us to be paid in full. Letting them go free, not holding them accountable for all the pain they have caused us. This action takes great grace because it e decaying in our body any longer.

We are opening ourselves up to love and trust again and to even dare to have hope in the future with joy in the Lord.

Romans 8:28, **"And we know that all things work together for good to them that love God, to them who are the called according to *his* purpose."**

To believe this verse we must believe that God

has allowed the loses in our lives, or the pains we are suffering, or the wrong doing which was done unto us. Yes, He does allow these things to enter our lives to help us grow in strength and faith in Him. He was using these events as growing tools and we sinned by not having the faith to trust our Father to take care of the situation whatever it may be. When we look at our bitter root and realize that God was there all the time we should start to see our way to a healing solution. We must acknowledge our sin for the lack of faith we had in God's presence in our life, trusting in God's wisdom and judgment in the matter.

Now you may not feel its fair for us to be the only one who needs to repent. But you see we're the one who is being harmed by the bitter root. The other party whoever they may be, are not even aware of our discomfort or sorrow and probably could care less that they have effected us as they have. So you see the only one who is hurt is us. We are the ones suffering the pain and the greatest pain of all is that of being separated from the close communion with God. Repentance is necessary for our lack of trust and faith in God's ability to handle the situation and take care of the other party for us. Trust God to deal with the other party. He will take care of them as only He can, touching them in His perfect way.

In the forgiving process you must review the

past, putting it into the proper perspective. Putting it all into its proper category within our mind and seeing it for what it really is now. Satan works on our minds and cripples so very many of God's children, using the memories of the past to bind us up. However, Christ set us free from the bonds of Satan and we have the victory over him for "Greater is the Holy Spirit within us than Satan who is in the world.

Now I would like to address a problem that some people have that is along the same line as the bitter root. These people are prone to having their feelings hurt very easily and seem to sit back and wait for someone to say or do something that will offend them. They are very easily offended and do not forgive readily. Have you ever met anyone like this?

Romans 14:7-13, **"For none of us liveth to himself, and no man dieth to himself. For whether we live, we live unto the Lord; and whether we die, we die unto the Lord: whether we live therefore, or die, we are the Lord's. For to this end Christ both died, and rose, and revived, that he might be Lord both of the dead and living. But why dost thou judge thy brother? or why dost thou set at nought thy brother? for we shall all stand before the judgment seat of Christ. For it is written,** *As* **I live, saith the Lord, every knee shall bow to me, and every tongue shall confess to God. So then every one of us shall give account**

of himself to God. Let us not therefore judge one another any more: but judge this rather, that no man put a stumblingblock or an occasion to fall in *his* brother's way."

Romans 14:19, **"Let us therefore follow after the things which make for peace, and things wherewith one may edify another."**

As we trust God to handle the entire situation including the other party, we can rest in the blessing of being back in close communion with our Lord once again. God rejoices when His children come to Him and ask for His help and trust Him to handle situations for us.

Trials and Tribulations

Some may feel that if they are living close to our Lord their lives will run along smoothly. This can be true to a certain extent. Trusting in our Lord keeps us at peace through faith while the world can be causing us havoc.

God said those of us who live godly shall suffer persecution - just as our "Hero's of Faith" did when they faced difficult times in their lives.

Hebrews 11:4-40, **"By faith Abel offered unto God a more excellent sacrifice than Cain, by which he obtained witness that he was righteous, God testifying of his gifts: and by it he being dead yet speaketh. By faith Enoch was translated that he should not see death; and was not found, because God had translated him: for before his translation he had this testimony, that he pleased God. But without faith** *it is* **impossible to please** *him***: for he that cometh to God must believe** *that* **he is, and that he is a rewarder of them that diligently seek him. By faith Noah, being warned of God of things not seen as yet, moved with fear, prepared an ark to the saving of his house; by the which he condemned the world, and became heir of the righteousness** which is by faith. By faith Abraham, when he was called to go out into a place which he should after receive for an inheritance, obeyed; and he went out, not knowing whither he went. By faith he sojourned in the land of promise, as *in* a strange country, dwelling in tabernacles with Isaac and Jacob, the heirs with him of the same promise: For he looked for a city which hath foundations, whose builder and maker *is* God. Through faith also Sara herself received strength to conceive seed, and was delivered of a child when she was past age, because she judged him faithful who had promised. Therefore sprang there even of one, and him as good as dead, *so many* as the stars of the sky in multitude, and as the sand which is by the sea shore innumerable. These all died in faith, not having received the promises, but having seen them afar off, and were persuaded of *them*, and embraced *them*, and confessed that they were strangers and pilgrims on the earth. For they that say such things declare plainly that they seek a country. And truly, if they had been mindful of that *country* from whence they came out, they might have had opportunity to have returned. But now they desire a better *country*, that is, an heavenly: wherefore God is not ashamed to be called their God: for he hath prepared for them a city. By faith

Trials and Tribulations

Abraham, when he was tried, offered up Isaac: and he that had received the promises offered up his only begotten *son*, Of whom it was said, That in Isaac shall thy seed be called: Accounting that God was able to raise *him* up, even from the dead; from whence also he received him in a figure. By faith Isaac blessed Jacob and Esau concerning things to come. By faith Jacob, when he was a dying, blessed both the sons of Joseph; and worshipped, *leaning* upon the top of his staff. By faith Joseph, when he died, made mention of the departing of the children of Israel; and gave commandment concerning his bones. By faith Moses, when he was born, was hid three months of his parents, because they saw *he was* a proper child; and they were not afraid of the king's commandment. By faith Moses, when he was come to years, refused to be called the son of Pharaoh's daughter; Choosing rather to suffer affliction with the people of God, than to enjoy the pleasures of sin for a season; Esteeming the reproach of Christ greater riches than the treasures in Egypt: for he had respect unto the recompence of the reward. By faith he forsook Egypt, not fearing the wrath of the king: for he endured, as seeing him who is invisible. Through faith he kept the passover, and the sprinkling of blood, lest he that destroyed the firstborn should touch them. By faith they passed through the Red sea as by dry *land*: which the Egyptians assaying to do were drowned. By faith the walls of Jericho fell down, after they were compassed about seven days. By faith the harlot Rahab perished not with them that believed not, when she had received the spies with peace. And what shall I more say? for the time would fail me to tell of Gedeon, and *of* Barak, and *of* Samson, and *of* Jephthae; *of* David also, and Samuel, and *of* the prophets: Who through faith subdued kingdoms, wrought righteousness, obtained promises, stopped the mouths of lions, Quenched the violence of fire, escaped the edge of the sword, out of weakness were made strong, waxed valiant in fight, turned to flight the armies of the aliens. Women received their dead raised to life again: and others were tortured, not accepting deliverance; that they might obtain a better resurrection: And others had trial of *cruel* mockings and scourgings, yea, moreover of bonds and imprisonment: They were stoned, they were sawn asunder, were tempted, were slain with the sword: they wandered about in sheepskins and goatskins; being destitute, afflicted, tormented; (Of whom the world was not worthy:) they wandered in deserts, and *in* mountains, and *in* dens and caves of the earth. And these all, having ob-

tained a good report through faith, received not the promise: God having provided some better thing for us, that they without us should not be made perfect."

I love to dwell on the thought "of whom the world was not worthy". How precious these hero's of faith are to us. The example they set for us to follow, "all having obtained a good report through faith". They all had a living testimony showing us how to live our lives by their examples. They were all flesh and bones just as we are. They did not have super spiritual strength to do all they did. They simply prayed to God and stayed close to Him following His commandments. We can live just such a faith filled life as well. But you see they did all this and still did not receive the promise they were striving for. Are we any more important than they were? Should our glory and reward be achieved here on earth or can we await it in heaven as they did?

Persecution will come to us who are faithful to God and His Word. He promises to always be with us to sustain us.

II Timothy 3:12, **"Yea, and all that will live godly in Christ Jesus shall suffer persecution."**

II Timothy 1:7-8, **"For God hath not given us the spirit of fear; but of power, and of love, and of a sound mind. Be not thou therefore ashamed of the testimony of our Lord, nor of me his pris-**

oner: but be thou partaker of the afflictions of the gospel according to the power of God;"

When persecution comes we should not be afraid for we are the children of God. Greater is He that is within us than he that is in the world. Our Lord is all powerful and nothing will touch us apart from His knowledge and we know that everything works together for our good for all of us who love Him.

Hold God in your hearts: and be ready always to give an answer to every man Romans 4:3-6, **"For what saith the scripture? Abraham believed God, and it was counted unto him for righteousness. Now to him that worketh is the reward not reckoned of grace, but of debt. But to him that worketh not, but believeth on him that justifieth the ungodly, his faith is counted for righteousness. Even as David also describeth the blessedness of the man, unto whom God imputeth righteousness without works,"**

Romans 8:18, **"For I reckon that the sufferings of this present time *are* not worthy *to be compared* with the glory which shall be revealed in us."**

Philippians 1:29, **"For unto you it is given in the behalf of Christ, not only to believe on him, but also to suffer for his sake;"**

I Peter 3:13-16, **"And who *is* he that will harm**

you, if ye be followers of that which is good? But and if ye suffer for righteousness' sake, happy *are ye*: and be not afraid of their terror, neither be troubled; But sanctify the Lord God in your hearts: and *be* ready always to *give* an answer to every man that asketh you a reason of the hope that is in you with meekness and fear: Having a good conscience; that, whereas they speak evil of you, as of evildoers, they may be ashamed that falsely accuse your good conversation in Christ."

I Peter 4:12-14, "**Beloved, think it not strange concerning the fiery trial which is to try you, as though some strange thing happened unto you: But rejoice, inasmuch as ye are partakers of Christ's sufferings; that, when his glory shall be revealed, ye may be glad also with exceeding joy. If ye be reproached for the name of Christ, happy *are ye*; for the spirit of glory and of God resteth upon you: on their part he is evil spoken of, but on your part he is glorified.**"

This is not to imply that our lives will be nothing but constant persecution. It just tells us that they will come and prepares us for readiness so we won't be caught off guard.

I John 5:4, "**For whatsoever is born of God overcometh the world: and this is the victory that overcometh the world, *even* our faith.**"

Christ loves us and our lives in our Lord will be

gifted with a sweet peace as we see the end drawing nearer. We know we can rest in true faith in Him. However, as the last days do come, it will be more and more bleak. Men will hate all that pertains to God. Anything remotely Christian will act as a conscience to their evil deeds and they will hate it. Our witness reveals their sinfulness and they can't take being shown what depraved men and women they really are. Even some people who are saved will dislike our Christian witness.

Romans 1:21-22, **"Because that, when they knew God, they glorified *him* not as God, neither were thankful; but became vain in their imaginations, and their foolish heart was darkened. Professing themselves to be wise, they became fools,"**

We must pray for the strength to be as great a witness of Christ as we can be in every area of our lives. As Christians, our standing for the Lord will really be obvious as our world grows darker.

Hebrews 10:23-24, **"Let us hold fast the profession of *our* faith without wavering; (for he *is* faithful that promised;) And let us consider one another to provoke unto love and to good works:"**

I Peter 5:8-9, **"Be sober, be vigilant; because your adversary the devil, as a roaring lion, walketh about, seeking whom he may devour:**

Whom resist stedfast in the faith, knowing that the same afflictions are accomplished in your brethren that are in the world."

You see again and again that our faith will be tested one way or another. Sometimes simply for our Christian stand and other times, because God wants to prune, and help us to grow stronger into mature children of the King. Persecution will be in our lives but we will never face it alone. God will always be with us, to support and give us all grace we need in every realm we need it. You see, He knows exactly what the trial is from the beginning of time and He already knows the outcome, so all we need to do is trust in Him and use the grace He so freely gives to all who will believe on Him. However, we should remember that God's purpose in pruning is to purge out the uncomely parts, to make us stronger and better vessels for the Masters use. God not only allows trials, but also designs them to be instrumental in the development of our character.

I Corinthians 15:58, **"Therefore, my beloved brethren, be ye stedfast, unmoveable, always abounding in the work of the Lord, forasmuch as ye know that your labour is not in vain in the Lord."** As we see in these verses, it is a great honour to go through trials for Christ's sake.

Ephesians 6:10-12, **"Finally, my brethren, be strong in the Lord, and in the power of his might.**

Put on the whole armour of God, that ye may be able to stand against the wiles of the devil. For we wrestle not against flesh and blood, but against principalities, against powers, against the rulers of the darkness of this world, against spiritual wickedness in high *places."*

With our armour in place and our trust in our God secure we should be ready to face the world. But there are times that the flesh has problems of its own. Sometimes our personal attributes need strengthening.

II Peter 1:3-10, **"According as his divine power hath given unto us all things that** *pertain* **unto life and godliness, through the knowledge of him that hath called us to glory and virtue: Whereby are given unto us exceeding great and precious promises: that by these ye might be partakers of the divine nature, having escaped the corruption that is in the world through lust. And beside this, giving all diligence, add to your faith virtue; and to virtue knowledge; And to knowledge temperance; and to temperance patience; and to patience godliness; And to godliness brotherly kindness; and to brotherly kindness charity. For if these things be in you, and abound, they make** *you that ye shall* **neither** *be* **barren nor unfruitful in the knowledge of our Lord Jesus Christ. But he that lacketh these things is blind, and can-**

not see afar off, and hath forgotten that he was purged from his old sins. Wherefore the rather, brethren, give diligence to make your calling and election sure: for if ye do these things, ye shall never fall:"

God never leaves us without protection, for as the trials come upon us, He exhorts us to put on His Armour. We will need this entire suit of armour to shield and completely protect us from the on slot of Satan's darts as we strive to serve our Lord. These trials will be a true test of our faith. It will call for us to stay close to our Lord and read our Bibles daily. Our reading and prayer time in our life is so very necessary in maintaining that close personal relationship with God. He is our all in all, without Him we are nothing but with Him "ye shall never fall."

Jude 1:3, **"Beloved, when I gave all diligence to write unto you of the common salvation, it was needful for me to write unto you, and exhort *you* that ye should earnestly contend for the faith which was once delivered unto the saints."**

Contending, much as a prize fighter would prepare and exercise for an upcoming boxing match, making himself ready in prime condition. Just so, we too in like manner are to contend or prepare for our battle. Only our fight is of a different sort - one of the heart, soul, and mind. We wage on different fronts against unseen forces. Satan has us so wrapped up in our worldly concerns that we don't even think about our Lord or His Church at times, let alone opening our Bibles to read them. We should have a Godly diligence rather than a worldly indulgence in our lives.

As we grow in grace and gain the use of the abilities listed above your Christian character will grow very strong. Learning more about the virtue of our Lord and His tremendous strength, will reinforce our faith as we trust Him to lead, provide, and protect us as we live for Him. When I feel a bit overwhelmed by this world I will often go to a special portion of scripture which gives me comfort and peace of mind.

Philippians 4:4-8, **"Rejoice in the Lord alway:** *and* **again I say, Rejoice. Let your moderation be known unto all men. The Lord** *is* **at hand. Be careful for nothing; but in every thing by prayer and supplication with thanksgiving let your requests be made known unto God. And the peace of God, which passeth all understanding, shall keep your hearts and minds through Christ Jesus. Finally, brethren, whatsoever things are true, whatsoever things** *are* **honest, whatsoever things** *are* **just, whatsoever things** *are* **pure, whatsoever things** *are* **lovely, whatsoever things** *are* **of good report; if** *there be* **any virtue, and if** *there be* **any praise, think on these things."**

As I read over these verses I meditate on each one. Dwelling on the meaning of each quality, the strength and power each adds to an individual. I refer to these verses as my cognitive therapy. They help me greatly to relax and find peace within. They settle me and remind me of my firm foundation- that being Christ our Lord.

Work as Unto the Lord

We are our Lord's children and when Christ went to the cross and died for our sins He paid our sin debt.

I Corinthians 6:20, **"For ye are bought with a price: therefore glorify God in your body, and in your spirit, which are God's."**

All who are saved by God's grace are no longer their own person. We owe our Saviour our life and should glorify Him in everything we do. This includes the workplace. When we go anywhere we should consider our time and energy is focused toward the Lord. We are the Lord's children and we should be a good witness in every aspect of our lives. We represent Christ on earth and we should ask ourselves what would Christ do. Be a living example in word and deed. This applies to us now more than ever before in history for our days are getting darker and our witness is more powerful now then it has ever been before.

Romans 12:11, **"Not slothful in business; fervent in spirit; serving the Lord;"**

Colossians 3:22-24, **"Servants, obey in all things *your* masters according to the flesh; not with eyeservice, as menpleasers; but in single-**

ness of heart, fearing God: And whatsoever ye do, do *it* heartily, as to the Lord, and not unto men; Knowing that of the Lord ye shall receive the reward of the inheritance: for ye serve the Lord Christ."

I Thessalonians 4:2-4 & 6, "**For ye know what commandments we gave you by the Lord Jesus. For this is the will of God,** *even* **your sanctification, that ye should abstain from fornication: That every one of you should know how to possess his vessel in sanctification and honour... That no** *man* **go beyond and defraud his brother in** *any* **matter: because that the Lord** *is* **the avenger of all such, as we also have forewarned you and testified."**

I Peter 2:18-25, "**Servants,** *be* **subject to** *your* **masters with all fear; not only to the good and gentle, but also to the froward. For this** *is* **thankworthy, if a man for conscience toward God endure grief, suffering wrongfully. For what glory** *is it*, **if, when ye be buffeted for your faults, ye shall take it patiently? but if, when ye do well, and suffer** *for it*, **ye take it patiently, this** *is* **acceptable with God. For even hereunto were ye called: because Christ also suffered for us, leaving us an example, that ye should follow his steps: Who did no sin, neither was guile found in his mouth: Who, when he was reviled, reviled not again;**

when he suffered, he threatened not; but committed *himself* to him that judgeth righteously: Who his own self bare our sins in his own body on the tree, that we, being dead to sins, should live unto righteousness: by whose stripes ye were healed. For ye were as sheep going astray; but are now returned unto the Shepherd and Bishop of your souls."

II Corinthians 8:21, "**Providing for honest things, not only in the sight of the Lord, but also in the sight of men.**"

This is also good as we go about our lives being a good example to the world as a whole. As we live godly we can tell others about Christ and what He did on the Cross for our sins.

If we had a bad testimony how could we ever tell others of Christ and His goodness or the plan of salvation. People would wonder where we had the right to say to them that they were sinners in need of a Saviour when we ourselves show such need.

II Corinthians 5:14-15, "**For the love of Christ constraineth us; because we thus judge, that if one died for all, then were all dead: And *that* he died for all, that they which live should not henceforth live unto themselves, but unto him which died for them, and rose again.**"

I Corinthians 6:19-20, "**What? know ye not that your body is the temple of the Holy Ghost** *which is* in you, which ye have of God, and ye are not your own? For ye are bought with a price: therefore glorify God in your body, and in your spirit, which are God's."

As we live for our Lord and stand for the truths in His Word we will come to appreciate Him and desire to live a godly life, a testimony for His honor and glory.

James 1:2-6, "**My brethren, count it all joy when ye fall into divers temptations; Knowing** *this*, **that the trying of your faith worketh patience. But let patience have** *her* **perfect work, that ye may be perfect and entire, wanting nothing. If any of you lack wisdom, let him ask of God, that giveth to all** *men* **liberally, and upbraideth not; and it shall be given him. But let him ask in faith, nothing wavering. For he that wavereth is like a wave of the sea driven with the wind and tossed.**"

James 2:14-26, "**What** *doth it* **profit, my brethren, though a man say he hath faith, and have not works? can faith save him? If a brother or sister be naked, and destitute of daily food, And one of you say unto them, Depart in peace, be** *ye* **warmed and filled; notwithstanding ye give them not those things which are needful to the body; what** *doth it* **profit? Even so faith, if it hath not works, is dead, being alone. Yea, a man may** say, Thou hast faith, and I have works: shew me thy faith without thy works, and I will shew thee my faith by my works. Thou believest that there is one God; thou doest well: the devils also believe, and tremble. But wilt thou know, O vain man, that faith without works is dead? Was not Abraham our father justified by works, when he had offered Isaac his son upon the altar? Seest thou how faith wrought with his works, and by works was faith made perfect? And the scripture was fulfilled which saith, Abraham believed God, and it was imputed unto him for righteousness: and he was called the Friend of God. Ye see then how that by works a man is justified, and not by faith only. Likewise also was not Rahab the harlot justified by works, when she had received the messengers, and had sent *them* out another way? For as the body without the spirit is dead, so faith without works is dead also."

Our Lord's Return

What would you do if you were told our Lord was to return one week from today and you had just seven days left on this earth to live for Him? Would you ask yourself questions about your righteous stand before God? Would you look to find any sin that might be lying between you and our Lord? Are you found living after the flesh in certain areas of your life?

Colossians 3:8-10, **"But now ye also put off all these; anger, wrath, malice, blasphemy, filthy communication out of your mouth. Lie not one to another, seeing that ye have put off the old man with his deeds; And have put on the new *man*, which is renewed in knowledge after the image of him that created him:"**

Romans 7:25, **"I thank God through Jesus Christ our Lord…"** So then with the, O that they were wise, that they understood this, that they would consider their latter end!

Have you been content in your life?

Philippians 4:11-13, **"Not that I speak in respect of want: for I have learned, in whatsoever state I am, *therewith* to be content. I know both how to be abased, and I know how to abound: ev-**

ery where and in all things I am instructed both to be full and to be hungry, both to abound and to suffer need. I can do all things through Christ which strengtheneth me."

II Timothy 3:1-7, **"This know also, that in the last days perilous times shall come. For men shall be lovers of their own selves, covetous, boasters, proud, blasphemers, disobedient to parents, unthankful, unholy, Without natural affection, trucebreakers, false accusers, incontinent, fierce, despisers of those that are good, Traitors, heady, highminded, lovers of pleasures more than lovers of God; Having a form of godliness, but denying the power thereof: from such turn away. For of this sort are they which creep into houses, and lead captive silly women laden with sins, led away with divers lusts, Ever learning, and never able to come to the knowledge of the truth."**

We would search our hearts to find any sin that might be within that would separate us from the Living God. We should ask Him to reveal unto us any sins that are in our lives that we are not aware of so we might repent of them and come before Him with a pure heart fervently desiring to serve Him.

In repentance of this we realize that God is the desire of our hearts.

From Deuteronomy 4:9, **"Only take heed to**

thyself, and keep thy soul diligently, lest thou forget the things which thine eyes have seen, and lest they depart from thy heart all the days of thy life: but teach them thy sons, and thy sons' sons;"

I Corinthians 2:5, "That your faith should not stand in the wisdom of men, but in the power of God."

Galatians 2:20, "I am crucified with Christ: nevertheless I live; yet not I, but Christ liveth in me: and the life which I now live in the flesh I live by the faith of the Son of God, who loved me, and gave himself for me."

Ephesians 2:8-10, "**For by grace are ye saved through faith; and that not of yourselves:** *it is* **the gift of God: Not of works, lest any man should boast. For we are his workmanship, created in Christ Jesus unto good works, which God hath before ordained that we should walk in them.**"

Life in Christ after repentance is glorious.

Ephesians 3:11-12, "**According to the eternal purpose which he purposed in Christ Jesus our Lord: In whom we have boldness and access with confidence by the faith of him.**"

Ephesians 3:17-19, "**That Christ may dwell in your hearts by faith; that ye, being rooted and grounded in love, May be able to comprehend with all saints what** *is* **the breadth, and length,** and depth, and height; And to know the love of Christ, which passeth knowledge, that ye might be filled with all the fulness of God."

Colossians 2:6-7, **"As ye have therefore received Christ Jesus the Lord,** *so* **walk ye in him: Rooted and built up in him, and stablished in the faith, as ye have been taught, abounding therein with thanksgiving."**

Knowing we are secure in our standing with our Lord we will turn our concern to our lost loved ones. We now realize how much time we have let pass without witnessing to theses people we hold so dear. People we know we do not want to be in heaven without. We Ask God to forgive us for not witnessing to them sooner and pray for His mercies in approaching them now.

Hebrews 6:11-12, **"And we desire that every one of you do shew the same diligence to the full assurance of hope unto the end: That ye be not slothful, but followers of them who through faith and patience inherit the promises."**

I Peter 5:6-7, **"Humble yourselves therefore under the mighty hand of God, that he may exalt you in due time: Casting all your care upon him; for he careth for you."**

We are to live by faith being guided by the truths in God's Word.

Proverbs 1:7, **"The fear of the LORD** *is* **the be-**

ginning of knowledge: *but* **fools despise wisdom and instruction."**

God's grace is so merciful as He leads and directs us. He asks that we live our lives holy and acceptable unto Him, presenting our bodies a living sacrifice. Now what does that mean? As we live our lives going about day by day, we are to put off our old bad habits. The ones that do not honor or glorify God. We should strive to do everything in our lives that would please our Lord, never bringing shame and reproach to His name. We are the only living example He has here on earth. Remember we are bought with a price. That price being the precious blood of our Lord Jesus Christ as He gave His life on the cross of Calvary, shedding His blood for our sins.

Romans 13:11, **"And that, knowing the time, that now** *it is* **high time to awake out of sleep: for now our salvation nearer than when we believed."**

We should tell our dear ones that Christ died on the Cross of Calvary for their sins, shedding His precious blood for the remission of those sins. Taking away our sins.

Matthew 26:28, **"For this is my blood of the new testament, which is shed for many for the remission of sins."**

Romans 6:23, **"For the wages of sin** *is* **death;**

but the gift of God *is* eternal life through Jesus Christ our Lord."

He gave His life for all those who would accept Him and believe that He is the Son of God who came to take away their sins. We have salvation in and through our Lord Jesus Christ.

I Thessalonians 5:9-10, **"For God hath not appointed us to wrath, but to obtain salvation by our Lord Jesus Christ, Who died for us, that, whether we wake or sleep, we should live together with him."**

Romans 10:9-11, **"That if thou shalt confess with thy mouth the Lord Jesus, and shalt believe in thine heart that God hath raised him from the dead, thou shalt be saved. For with the heart man believeth unto righteousness; and with the mouth confession is made unto salvation. For the scripture saith, Whosoever believeth on him shall not be ashamed."**

Before we felt our Lord's return so eminent, we were reserved about talking about Christ and witnessing personally to others. However, now that our time is so short we realize that our reservations, shyness or the fear about telling others about Christ is gone and we can't wait to tell the blessed story of Christ gift of salvation. Praying that God's mercy will be present and working in our loved ones lives. For their salvation is desperately important to us now that we know time has run out.

Matthew 6:30, **"Wherefore, if God so clothe the grass of the field, which to day is, and to morrow is cast into the oven, *shall he* not much more *clothe* you, O ye of little faith?"**

But Wait!-Why do we feel time hasn't run out? Who among us know we have a week of tomorrows before our Lord returns. The news every night reads like Revelation coming to pass. None of us know we have long before our Lord returns so why do we still wait, putting off the witness that means the most in the world to us? Let us not tarry any longer, but share our love of Christ now while there is time because there won't be an advance warning when He truly does return. Share with our loved ones all that can be theirs in and through our Lord Jesus Christ.

Jeremiah 29:11-13, **"For I know the thoughts that I think toward you, saith the LORD, thoughts of peace, and not of evil, to give you an expected end. Then shall ye call upon me, and ye shall go and pray unto me, and I will hearken unto you. And ye shall seek me, and find *me*, when ye shall search for me with all your heart."**

I Corinthians 2:9, **"But as it is written, Eye hath not seen, nor ear heard, neither have entered into the heart of man, the things which God hath prepared for them that love him."**

Romans 5:1-2, "Therefore being justified by faith, we have peace with God through our Lord Jesus Christ: By whom also we have access by faith into this grace wherein we stand, and rejoice in hope of the glory of God."

John 16:33, "These things I have spoken unto you, that in me ye might have peace. In the world ye shall have tribulation: but be of good cheer; I have overcome the world."

Titus 3:1-8, "Put them in mind to be subject to principalities and powers, to obey magistrates, to be ready to every good work, To speak evil of no man, to be no brawlers, *but* gentle, shewing all meekness unto all men. For we ourselves also were sometimes foolish, disobedient, deceived, serving divers lusts and pleasures, living in malice and envy, hateful, *and* hating one another. But after that the kindness and love of God our Saviour toward man appeared, Not by works of righteousness which we have done, but according to his mercy he saved us, by the washing of regeneration, and renewing of the Holy Ghost; Which he shed on us abundantly through Jesus Christ our Saviour; That being justified by his grace, we should be made heirs according to the hope of eternal life. *This is* a faithful saying, and these things I will that thou affirm constantly, that they which have believed in God might be careful to maintain good works. These things are good and profitable unto men."

America Land of the Free?

This segment is a fresh one touchy to the nerves. Just recently our country lost a great deal of its freedom through a signature on a piece of paper. It was backed by a group of people who would not listen to those who voted them into office. The people of America were not listened to but rather were deliberately ignored. The Constitution is being changed or ignored and by each signature on paper our President moves our Nation one step closer to Socialism or worse. Now how are we to react to these happenings? Yes indeed we are to pray like we have never prayed before for our country and our liberties. But we are also to trust and rest in our Lord also throughout this entire ordeal. To the flesh it may appear as if the world as we know it is falling apart. Indeed, our independence is being robbed from us and big government is taking over every aspect of our lives. However we can rest assured in our God that He has all things in control and that nothing is happening without His knowledge and permission.

Romans 13:1-7, **"Let every soul be subject unto the higher powers. For there is no power but of God: the powers that be are ordained of**

God. Whosoever therefore resisteth the power, resisteth the ordinance of God: and they that resist shall receive to themselves damnation. For rulers are not a terror to good works, but to the evil. Wilt thou then not be afraid of the power? do that which is good, and thou shalt have praise of the same: For he is the minister of God to thee for good. But if thou do that which is evil, be afraid; for he beareth not the sword in vain: for he is the minister of God, a revenger to *execute* wrath upon him that doeth evil. Wherefore *ye* must needs be subject, not only for wrath, but also for conscience sake. For for this cause pay ye tribute also: for they are God's ministers, attending continually upon this very thing. Render therefore to all their dues: tribute to whom tribute *is due*; custom to whom custom; fear to whom fear; honour to whom honour."

God has all power in Heaven and earth which includes all the governments that reign. We are to obey these powers that God has put into place and give respect to the office. But when it comes time we can vote them out and vote for more honorable men if there are any to be found. We can write our Heads of State and make our feelings and desires known. We can let them know in a peaceful manner that what they are doing is not for the betterment of the people but we must never become violent in any way. Peaceful demonstrations like those of the "Tea Parties" are acceptable and let Washington know that we want them to stand for our Constitutional rights. Things have to get bad before our Lord returns for us. As we read the Bible we will not find the United States mentioned. Why is that do you suppose? Perhaps it's because we are no longer a nation to be recognized as having power. No longer the number one nation in the world, but bankrupt and in such need that we could be a third world country in no time at all.

As I said before, we are not to worry at all for God has all of this under control and we will all be fine under His marvelous care. We will have to go back to our Great Grandparents ways of gardening for our foods and living closer to home. When our elderly are no longer able to live on their own they will have to move in with their children as they did in years gone by. There will have to be a great deal of down-sizing, from the size of our homes to the number of our cars. The trips to the fashion stores will few and far between. Adjustment will be the theme of the day and we will be able to do it all just fine with our Lord's great grace and strength in our lives. Reading our Bibles will be more precious to us all. We should not be surprised if our churches and Pastors all come under attack for preaching the Word in truth - which the world calls hate crimes.

Any time we tell the truth about gay rights, abortion, constitutional liberties and religious freedoms.

This may all sound very bleak and horrid thinking of our country falling to such a level but we must keep our minds in the right direction. Remember God knows all about our countries state of being. He's still on the Throne and ready to help us all as we seek His face and ask Him for all the grace we are in need of. He loves His children dearly and will never leave us alone. Our country has to go through some hard times and we will go through them for a while until He takes us home to be with Him for eternity.

Psalms 22:27-28, **"All the ends of the world shall remember and turn unto the LORD: and all the kindreds of the nations shall worship before thee. For the kingdom *is* the LORD'S: and he *is* the governor among the nations."**

We all must strive to endure to the end through faith in our Lord Jesus Christ who will be returning for us soon.

Matthew 10:22, **"And ye shall be hated of all *men* for my name's sake: but he that endureth to the end shall be saved."**

I Corinthians 13:4-13, **"Charity suffereth long, *and* is kind; charity envieth not; charity vaunteth not itself, is not puffed up, Doth not behave itself unseemly, seeketh not her own,** is not easily provoked, thinketh no evil; Rejoiceth not in iniquity, but rejoiceth in the truth; Beareth all things, believeth all things, hopeth all things, endureth all things. Charity never faileth: but whether *there be* prophecies, they shall fail; whether *there be* tongues, they shall cease; whether *there be* knowledge, it shall vanish away. For we know in part, and we prophesy in part. But when that which is perfect is come, then that which is in part shall be done away. When I was a child, I spake as a child, I understood as a child, I thought as a child: but when I became a man, I put away childish things. For now we see through a glass, darkly; but then face to face: now I know in part; but then shall I know even as also I am known. And now abideth faith, hope, charity, these three; but the greatest of these *is* charity."

II Timothy 2:3-5, "Thou therefore endure hardness, as a good soldier of Jesus Christ. No man that warreth entangleth himself with the affairs of *this* life; that he may please him who hath chosen him to be a soldier. And if a man also strive for masteries, *yet* is he not crowned, except he strive lawfully."

James 1:11-12, "For the sun is no sooner risen with a burning heat, but it withereth the grass, and the flower thereof falleth, and the grace of the fashion of it perisheth: so also shall the rich man fade away in his ways. Blessed *is* the man that endureth temptation: for when he is tried, he shall receive the crown of life, which the Lord hath promised to them that love him."

James 5:7-12, "**Be patient therefore, brethren, unto the coming of the Lord. Behold, the husbandman waiteth for the precious fruit of the earth, and hath long patience for it, until he receive the early and latter rain. Be ye also patient; stablish your hearts: for the coming of the Lord draweth nigh. Grudge not one against another, brethren, lest ye be condemned: behold, the judge standeth before the door. Take, my brethren, the prophets, who have spoken in the name of the Lord, for an example of suffering affliction, and of patience. Behold, we count them happy which endure. Ye have heard of the patience of Job, and have seen the end of the Lord; that the Lord is very pitiful, and of tender mercy. But above all things, my brethren, swear not, neither by heaven, neither by the earth, neither by any other oath: but let your yea be yea; and *your* nay, nay; lest ye fall into condemnation.**"

Our Pathway Home

I've covered several areas in which we may have sin in an effort to help us all to better prepare our repentant hearts, ready to trust our Lord by faith. Perhaps I haven't mentioned your particular problem but whatever it may be, if you are not right with our Lord and able to find peace and rest for your soul please search your hearts and minds and ask God what separates you from Him. He will reveal to you what the problem is, than you can acknowledge the sin and repent.

Deuteronomy 7:9, **"Know therefore that the LORD thy God, he *is* God, the faithful God, which keepeth covenant and mercy with them that love him and keep his commandments to a thousand generations;"**

The path less taken is the one which draws us nearer to God. For indeed it is a hard path to take because it calls for deep soul searching and revealing of sin in our lives. Than we must not only recognize the sin but accept it as our own and repent of that sin. True repentance is to turn completely away from that sin and leave it behind us, never to allow it in our lives again.

Colossians 1:20, **"And, having made peace**

through the blood of his cross, by him to reconcile all things unto himself; by him, *I say,* whether *they be* things in earth, or things in heaven."

To maintain a repentant life we must read our Bibles every day and have a close prayer life with our Lord. This is the only way we can learn of Him and truly know who our Father in Heaven is. Reading His promises to us and learning of all the miraculous things He has done and can do for us as well, will help our faith to grow and become stronger.

As we read our Bibles and pray to God, the world cannot dwell within our hearts and minds. Learning how much He loves us, what He desires of our lives, and the blessings that will be ours if we remain close to Him is the greatest gift of all. But in order to gain this closeness the world must be removed.

What comes out of our lives is what we put into it. You've heard the saying, "you are what you eat". Well the same is true here for what we put into ourselves is what will come out. If we read worldly writings and watch worldly shows and listen to worldly music it leaves us with worldly thoughts and actions. If we read Christian literature and live around other Christians we will act and sound like Christians,

John 16:33, **"These things I have spoken unto you, that in me ye might have peace. In the world ye shall have tribulation: but be of good cheer; I have overcome the world."**

Our Pathway Home

As you read God's Word and pray, meditate on just who and what God is-The Holy One who has all power in Heaven and earth. As we come to realize that He is all powerful we can learn to trust Him with any problem no matter how large or small - I mean literally. We ladies have the home as our realm and things pertaining to our home matters to us. God knows this and He is very happy to help us in all areas of our personal lives. No area is too small or insignificant for us not to concern Him. I remember a time when we were rather low on funds and we had a fellowship coming up. I was to make food for this fellowship and our pantry was nearly bear. So I went to our Father and asked for a recipe to make up something nice with what little I had. When I went to sleep that night I had a dream of how to make up a certain dish and when I made it, it turned out wonderfully. God takes care of all things for us. Even little things are important to Him.

We can trust our Heavenly Father who can do more than we can hope or think. Read His Word and learn of all the miracles He brought to pass. Get to know Him so that trusting Him so deeply will become second nature to us.

Job 22:21, **"Acquaint now thyself with him, and be at peace: thereby good shall come unto thee."**

The Fruit of the Spirit is very helpful when we

develop them fully. Enhancing these nine fruit into our lives make us stronger Christians with a more spiritual outlook. Contrariwise the fruit of the flesh are to be noted and we will strive to overcome our tendency toward them. The following is the listing of the Fruit of the Flesh and Spirit along with their meanings.

Fruits of the Flesh: Galatians 5:16-23
 1. Adultery; adultery
 2. Fornication; harlotry (also adultery and incest) idolatry
 3. Uncleanness; impure, foul, unclean
 4. Lasciviousness; licentiousness (dissolute; immoral) filthy, and wantonness (unrestrained, wild reckless, heartless, malicious, dissolute, an unrestrained or dissolute person)
 5. Idolatry; image worship or heathen god and worship of such.
 6. Witchcraft; druggist, medication, Pharmacy, sorcery, magic
 7. Hatred; hostility, a reason for opposition, enmity
 8. Variance; wrangling, contention, debate, strife, quarrel
 9. Emulations; heat – "zeal", jealousy, malice, envy, fervent, mind, indignation
 10 Wrath; passion, fierceness, indignation, wrath

11. Strife; intrigue, faction, contention (ious), strife
12. Seditions; disunion, sedition, (incitement of rebellion) dissension (violent disagreement), strife, discord, division
13. Heresies; a choice, a party of disunion, sect
14. Envyings; ill will, as distractions; jealousy, spite
15. Murders; to slay, murder / to be slain with, slaughter
16. Drunkenness; an intoxicant, intoxication
17. Revellings; a carousing (as if letting loose), rioting

Fruits of the Spirit:
1. Love; affection or benevolence (manifesting a desire to so well, charity
2. Joy; cheerfulness, calm delight, gladness, rest
3. Peace; prosperity, one, peace, quietness, rest
4. Longsuffering; forbearance, fortitude (the power to endure pain hardship), patience,
5. Gentleness; usefulness, excellence (in character or demeanor), good (ness), kindness
6. Goodness; virtue or beneficence
7. Faith; persuasion, conviction, reliance upon Christ for Salvation; truthfulness of God, constancy in such profession assurance, belief, fidel-

ity (faithfulness, loyalty, accuracy, exactness)
8. Meekness; gentleness, humility-humble
9. Temperance; self-control; temperance (moderation, kept or keeping within reasonable limits)

Against such there is no law.

As children of God we possess these qualities. We may have to develop them more fully. It is God's desire that we use these "Fruit of the Spirit" to their fullest and His Holy Spirit will lead and direct us, giving us each the strength we're in need of to obtain our goals.

Titus 2:11-12, **"For the grace of God that bringeth salvation hath appeared to all men, Teaching us that, denying ungodliness and worldly lusts, we should live soberly, righteously, and godly, in this present world;"**

We must strive to maintain these qualities in our daily lives. If we serve the flesh we will not desire to commune with God. Reading our Bibles regularly and praying are essential for building our faith. As we look over the definitions of the fruit of the flesh, we can identify any that we see we have some weaknesses toward. It is very important to maintain our closeness with our Lord so much more as we see the day of His return drawing nearer.

I Peter 4:7-10, **"But the end of all things is**

at hand: be ye therefore sober, and watch unto prayer. And above all things have fervent charity among yourselves: for charity shall cover the multitude of sins. Use hospitality one to another without grudging. As every man hath received the gift, *even so* minister the same one to another, as good stewards of the manifold grace of God."

Matthew 24:12-13, "**And because iniquity shall abound, the love of many shall wax cold. But he that shall endure unto the end, the same shall be saved.**"

Iniquity-(evil ways)

We can feel this coldness about us even now in our Christian realm. People are becoming more easily discouraged. Rather than being more excited about the Day of our Lord drawing near, people are becoming more depressed.

Ephesians 6:10-12, "**Finally, my brethren, be strong in the Lord, and in the power of his might. Put on the whole armour of God, that ye may be able to stand against the wiles of the devil. For we wrestle not against flesh and blood, but against principalities, against powers, against the rulers of the darkness of this world, against spiritual wickedness in high *places*.**"

Hebrews 11:1-3, "**Now faith is the substance of things hoped for, the evidence of things not seen. For by it the elders obtained a good report.**

Through faith we understand that the worlds were framed by the word of God, so that things which are seen were not made of things which do appear."

How do we go about t if it's within His timetable for us.

A good example of asked and answered prayer is found in Malachi 3:10, **"Bring ye all the tithes into the storehouse, that there may be meat in mine house, and prove me now herewith, saith the LORD of hosts, if I will not open you the windows of heaven, and pour you out a blessing, that *there shall* not *be room* enough *to receive it.*"**

I love this verse because God challenges us to prove Him, test Him and see if He doesn't bless us for our faithfulness as in this example of tithing. I find it wonderful that our Father puts forth this challenge to us as an invitation to test Him and His promises that He has given us in His Word.

Faith is a reliance upon Christ and the truthfulness of God.

Hebrews 6:18, **"That by two immutable things, in which *it was* impossible for God to lie, we might have a strong consolation, who have fled for refuge to lay hold upon the hope set before us:"**

Hebrews 10:23, **"Let us hold fast the profession of *our* faith without wavering; (for he *is***

faithful that promised;)"

God cannot lie. Putting our trust in Him for our care and well being is a safe and wise thing to do for we are His children and He wants nothing but the very best for us.

The problem lies in the fact that His children don't realize that following God's commandments and doing the will of our Father is the very best thing for us personally. Our flesh darkens our eyes.

Romans 6:15-17, **"What then? shall we sin, because we are not under the law, but under grace? God forbid. Know ye not, that to whom ye yield yourselves servants to obey, his servants ye are to whom ye obey; whether of sin unto death, or of obedience unto righteousness? But God be thanked, that ye were the servants of sin, but ye have obeyed from the heart that form of doctrine which was delivered you."**

Ephesians 2:1-10, **"And you *hath he quickened,* who were dead in trespasses and sins; Wherein in time past ye walked according to the course of this world, according to the prince of the power of the air, the spirit that now worketh in the children of disobedience: Among whom also we all had our conversation in times past in the lusts of our flesh, fulfilling the desires of the flesh and of the mind; and were by nature the children of wrath, even as others. But God, who is rich in** mercy, for his great love wherewith he loved us, Even when we were dead in sins, hath quickened us together with Christ, (by grace ye are saved;) And hath raised *us* up together, and made *us* sit together in heavenly *places* in Christ Jesus: That in the ages to come he might shew the exceeding riches of his grace in *his* kindness toward us through Christ Jesus. For by grace are ye saved through faith; and that not of yourselves: *it is* the gift of God: Not of works, lest any man should boast. For we are his workmanship, created in Christ Jesus unto good works, which God hath before ordained that we should walk in them."**

If we continually followed our Lord and His Word, living a life honoring Him, we would find ourselves dwelling in peace and harmony.

Romans 14:17, **"For the kingdom of God is not meat and drink; but righteousness, and peace, and joy in the Holy Ghost."**

Everyone wants peace and tranquility in their busy, stress filled lives. This is possible only in and through our Lord. So many people relate peace and joy to a time or place where you can find tranquility. Away from the fast pace of our busy lives. They associate peace and joy with sound and motion. But true peace and joy are not in situations. They are found within and are God given. They have nothing to do with the circumstances around us. Our world could be crumbling down about us and we still can have the peace that passes all understanding.

This type of peace and joy come because we trust and have faith in our Father to take care of all situations no matter what may come along. Trust Him knowing that even if a problem does touch us it is with God's knowledge and it's for a very good purpose. Resting in our Lord in all things whatever they may be because we trust the wisdom of God's care over us and know He will never leave nor forsake us. We are never alone.

Walk on the Water

Faith is not seen but it is felt in and through us by the Holy Spirit. By trusting in our Lord with our very soul and knowing He will never leave us nor forsake us.

Hebrews 13:5-6, **"Let your conversation be without covetousness; and be content with such things as ye have: for he hath said, I will never leave thee, nor forsake thee. So that we may boldly say, The Lord is my helper, and I will not fear what man shall do unto me."**

Philippians 3:7-9, **"But what things were gain to me, those I counted loss for Christ. Yea doubtless, and I count all things but loss for the excellency of the knowledge of Christ Jesus my Lord: for whom I have suffered the loss of all things, and do count them but dung, that I may win Christ, And be found in him, not having mine own righteousness, which is of the law, but that which is through the faith of Christ, the righteousness which is of God by faith:"**

All that we may go through for our Lord should be a joy and privilege to be counted worthy to suffer for the sake of Christ, for He is our example. Not all will be accounted worthy. Only those who have kept the faith and strive to diligently serve Him. A living faith with our eyes on God, knowing all things are on a solid foundation in Him even while the world crumbles about us.

I Timothy 1:14, **"And the grace of our Lord was exceeding abundant with faith and love which is in Christ Jesus."**

Romans 1:17, **"For therein is the righteousness of God revealed from faith to faith: as it is written, The just shall live by faith."**

I John 5:4, **"For whatsoever is born of God overcometh the world: and this is the victory that overcometh the world, *even* our faith."**

To walk on the water as Peter did take's a great deal of faith. If Peter had kept his eyes on Christ he could have walked directly to Him. Faith is such a joyful thing when we are that close to our Lord. The inner joy and peace is overwhelming when we have such a close personal relationship with our Lord.

That is why it is so sad that Peter took his eyes off Christ. For you see, when he did he lost sight of all that Christ had for him. All he could see were the stormy seas and waves that were beating about him.

He is an example for us today as we walk about in our daily lives. When we keep our eyes on Christ, reading our Bibles daily and praying very regularly we stay in close contact. Learning of the many promises and truths, and trusting in them in our hearts.

We must guard against taking our eyes off Christ. That's when we will sink into the deep sea of this world's troubles.

It's all so simple when we seek forgiveness for our sins and repent, drawing closer to our Lord once again. We should keep our relationship open and fresh, free of sin that so easily besets us. The harmony with our Lord is certainly worth the effort in this flesh that it takes to maintain this close union. The peace and joy that can be ours even while the world and our government goes into chaos. Nothing can be anymore beautiful than the blissful fellowship shared continually with God.

It won't be very long and our Lord will return. What a glorious day that will be.

Psalms 29:11, "**The LORD will give strength unto his people; the LORD will bless his people with peace.**"

Colossians 3:15, "**And let the peace of God rule in your hearts, to the which also ye are called in one body; and be ye thankful.**"

Ecclesiastes 12:13-14, "**Let us hear the conclusion of the whole matter: Fear God, and keep his commandments: for this *is* the whole *duty* of man. For God shall bring every work into judgment, with every secret thing, whether *it be* good, or whether *it be* evil.**"

References

All Bible references taken from "Micro Bible Library," Windows 95 & Above, Version 6, King James Version

All definitions taken from "Strong's Exhaustive Concordance of the Bible"

Janet E. Channell
janetchannell@yahoo.com